THAT'S ONE FOR THE BOOK...

unwritten rules for life

(now written!!!)

First published in the United Kingdom in 2020
by Cavalcade Books

www.cavalcadebooks.com

© The Three Witches 2020

ISBN 978-1-8381490-4-8

Authors' note: This book comprises rules for life we've collected over the years and tried our best to live by! We can't claim to be the inventors of all of them. Some of them, we're sure, came to us via friends and family, and some may have come from ideas we once heard somewhere and have forgotten from where. So, thanks go out as applicable to all our friends and families for their help in compiling this book, even though they, like us, are to remain anonymous.

"Don't take life too seriously. You'll never get out alive."
Bugs Bunny

RULE 1

DON'T TRUST MEN WHO DRINK TEA.

(We realise this means most of the male population!)

RULE 2

ALWAYS WEAR COMFY SHOES TO SHOP TILL YOU DROP!

RULE 3

DON'T GO OUT WITH A BLOKE WITH LONGER HAIR THAN YOU.

RULE 4A

DON'T WEAR PVC OR LEATHER ON A HOT NIGHT.

RULE 4B

DON'T USE TALC AND WEAR HOLD UP STOCKINGS.

RULE 4C

PUT YOUR COWBOY BOOTS INSIDE THE LEGS OF YOUR JEANS BEFORE PUTTING YOUR JEANS ON.

(We admit these three are of their time, but fashions do have a habit of returning . . .)

RULE 5

CHOCOLATE ANSWERS MOST PROBLEMS.

RULE 6

ASK YOURSELF ... WHAT'S THE WORST THAT COULD HAPPEN?

RULE 7

CIDER'S CHEAP AND IT WORKS . . .

(although not as cheap as it used to be)

RULE 8

THINGS NEVER HAPPEN WHEN YOU EXPECT THEM TO.

RULE 9

IF YOU ARE ASKING YOURSELF "WHAT WOULD HAPPEN IF . . . ?" DON'T DO IT!

RULE 10

IF IN DOUBT, TURN LEFT.

RULE 11

DON'T WEAR A SHORT BLACK SKIRT WITH BARE LEGS.

RULE 12

IF IT'S AFTER 2AM, IT DOESN'T MATTER – IT'S NOT REAL TIME!

RULE 13

IT'S NOT OVER TILL THE FAT LADY SINGS
– AND SHE'S NOT SINGING!

RULE 14

FINISH THINGS OR THEY'LL GET YOU IN THE END — SOMETIME.

RULE 15

GO TO DOGS, BUT LET CATS COME TO YOU.

RULE 16

SHAVING AND MATCHING UNDERWEAR ARE ESSENTIAL FOR A HOT, HOT DATE.

RULE 17

Shop till you drop,
dance till you fall over.

RULE 18

LIFE'S TOO SHORT TO MAKE YOUR OWN PICKLED ONIONS.

(And BEWARE making jam is dangerous!)

RULE 19

IF YOU DON'T WANT TO GET ROPE BURN, LET GO.

RULE 20

THERE WILL ALWAYS BE SOMEONE WITH A DIFFERENT OPINION TO YOU.

RULE 21

PEOPLE WHO WALK IN THE MIDDLE OF THE ROAD GET RUN OVER.

RULE 22

DON'T PUT ANYTHING ON SOCIAL MEDIA THAT YOU WOULDN'T WANT PAINTED ON A SHEET AND HUNG ON A BUSY ROUNDABOUT.

RULE 23

IF YOU GO OUT WITH YOUR FRIENDS,
YOU GO HOME WITH YOUR FRIENDS!

RULE 24

CHECK YOUR KNICKERS OR SOCKS AREN'T STILL IN YOUR JEANS BEFORE YOU PUT THEM BACK ON IN THE MORNING.

RULE 25

DON'T TRY SHOES ON WHEN YOUR FEET ARE HOT – THEY MAY NOT FIT LATER.

(And don't kick your shoes off under the table of a restaurant, unless you like walking home barefoot!)

RULE 26

IF YOU NEED TO LEAVE A PUB QUICKLY, SAY TO YOUR FRIEND, "IS THAT A FISH AT THE BOTTOM OF YOUR GLASS?"

(The correct response to this is to say, "I don't know. I'll have a look," and drink up quickly!)

RULE 27

TATTOOS NEED MUCH THOUGHT AND THEN A LITTLE MORE THOUGHT – IN ADVANCE!

(Consider what it will look like when you're 75.)

RULE 28

ALL TIME PASSES EVENTUALLY.

RULE 29

TRYING JEANS ON TAKES THE FUN OUT OF SHOPPING.

RULE 30

IF YOU ARE NOT SURE ABOUT A BLOKE, WEAR YOUR OLD/BIG KNICKERS – IT MIGHT STOP YOU DOING SOMETHING YOU REGRET LATER.

RULE 31

LOOK BACK, BUT DON'T STARE!

RULE 32

ALWAYS MAKE SURE YOU HAVE SOMEONE IN YOUR LIFE YOU CAN PHONE AT 3 O'CLOCK IN THE MORNING IF YOU NEED THEM.

(Our numbers are . . .)

RULE 33

FOOTBALL (OTHER SPORTS ALSO APPLY) IS SOMETHING YOU JUST HAVE TO ACCEPT AND LIVE YOUR LIFE AROUND.

RULE 34

THINGS ALWAYS SEEM BETTER AND MORE ACHIEVABLE IN THE MORNING.

OR

THINGS ALWAYS SEEM BETTER AND MORE ACHIEVABLE AFTER DARK.

(Choose which one applies to you!)

RULE 35

LIFE IS BETTER IN BAMBOO UNDERWEAR.

(Google it - it's not just for yoga, you know!)

RULE 36

NEVER DROP A SUGARY SWEET
INTO A CAN OF COKE!

RULE 37

ALL MEN ARE GITS – SOME MEN ARE JUST BIGGER GITS THAN OTHERS!

RULE 38

IF A CAKE IN THE CAFÉ LOOKS LIKE IT'S BEEN UNDER THE GLASS DOME FOR A WHILE, IT'S PROBABLY BETTER TO HAVE CRISPS!

RULE 39

ALWAYS CHECK THE LID'S PROPERLY ON SOMETHING BEFORE YOU SHAKE IT.

(This applies to relationships as well as food/drink.)

RULE 40

BEWARE OF CHOOSING BOOKS (AND MEN) BY THEIR COVERS.

RULE 41

IT WILL BE ALRIGHT IN THE END —
IF IT'S NOT ALRIGHT, IT'S NOT
THE END!

AND FINALLY . . .

RULE 42

YOU WON'T THINK IT WILL EVER HAPPEN TO YOU (WE DIDN'T THINK IT WOULD HAPPEN TO US – WE STILL DON'T), BUT YOU WILL GET OLD ONE DAY ... MAKE SURE YOU HAVE SOMETHING TO LOOK BACK ON AND TALK ABOUT, AGAIN AND AGAIN!

These last pages are left intentionally blank for you to add your own rules to. We don't, or ever will, claim to know everything, and we definitely didn't always make the right decisions. If we had, we would have no stories to reminisce over and we wouldn't have written this book!

The Three Witches

www.ingramcontent.com/pod-product-compliance
Lightning Source LLC
Chambersburg PA
CBHW081357080526
44588CB00016B/2524